M000284392

THE HISTORY OF FARTING

BY
DR. BENJAMIN BART

SHELTER HARBOR PRESS
NEW YORK

First hardcover edition published in 2014 by Shelter Harbor Press

Originally published in Great Britain in 1995 by
Michael O'Mara Books Limited
9 Lion Yard
Tremadoc Road
London SW4 7NQ

Copyright © 1993 by Herron Publications Pty. Limited

Published by arrangement with Herron Publications Pty. Limited, Australia

All rights reserved. No part of this publication may be reproduced, stored in a retrieval system, or transmitted, in any form or by any means, electronic, mechanical, photocopying, recording, or otherwise, without prior written permission from the publisher. For permissions and other queries to info@shelterharborpress.com or write to:

SHELTER HARBOR PRESS
603 West 115th Street, Suite 163
New York, New York 10025

Cataloging-in-Publication Data has been applied for and may be obtained from the Library of Congress.

ISBN 978-1-62795-005-3

Printed and bound in China

10 9 8 7 6 5 4 3 2 1

THIS BOOK began as a collection of rhymes discovered in an inner drawer of a cedar chest left to me by my grandmother, Emily, widow of the late and hardly lamented Sir Gustave Bart, surgeon-general in the Prince of Wales Light Horse at the time of Beersheba, whose most frequently given medical advice to soldier and settler alike was: "Treat yourself to a good fart!" Why my grandmother, a gentle person who used lavender water and large quantities of potpourri to mask her own flatal indiscretions, kept these peculiar writings can only be guessed at, and perhaps, it has occurred to me, she carted the cedar chest around with her in complete ignorance of its unsettling contents.

When it came into my possession many years ago, however, I decided my grandfather's passion should not be allowed to fade into nothingness, as it were, and since then I have added from time to time to the collection, bringing it, I trust, a more modern bouquet. All of this was for my private entertainment and enjoyment, however, until one day a chance conversation with a highly decorated (and decorous) adviser to the Australian Literature Board persuaded me that the Bart Collection, as I had begun to refer to it, was part of the cultural heritage of this great country and deserved and even demanded a broader and more appreciative audience.

To that end, we have committed the Bart Collection to print, in hope and understanding that it will lead some of you, at least, to more richly fruitful and satisfying lives.

As I recall my grandfather saying to me one day as he dangled me on his knee in the garden overlooking the bean plantation he established in later life in a distant, misty valley of the Blue Mountains: "Benjamin, my boy, never be afraid to drop a good fart." To his memory, then, is this great work dedicated.

Benjamin Bart
Kirribilli, 1993

CONTENTS

CHAPTER 1

INTRODUCING THE FART

The *Macquarie Dictionary*
FART (Colloq.) -n. 1. an emission of wind from the anus, esp. an audible one. 2. a foolish or ineffectual person.-v.i. 3. to emit wind from the anus. 4. to behave stupidly or waste time (fol. by around or about). [ME ferten, OE feortan, c. OHG ferzen]

EVERYONE farts, admit it or not. Kings fart; Queens fart. Edward Lear, the 19th-century English landscape painter, wrote affectionately of a favorite farting Duchess who gave enormous dinner parties attended by the cream of society. One night she let out a ripper and quick as a flash she turned her gaze to her stoic butler, standing, as always, behind her. "Hawkins!" she cried. "Hawkins, stop that!" "Certainly, your Grace," he replied with unhurried dignity. "Which way did it go?"

St. Augustine claims to have seen someone in such control of his backside that he could break wind at will and follow the tone of verses spoken to him. Michael Eyquem de Montaigne warned: "God alone knows how many times our bellies, by the refusal of one single fart, have brought us to the door of an agonizing death. May the Emperor who gave us the freedom to fart where we like, also give us the power to do so."

The contemporary danger of holding back, as they say, is commemorated on a gravestone in a tiny cemetery in the town of Stanley on the north-west coast of Tasmania, birthplace of former prime minister Joe Lyons. In carved stone it thus records:

Where-ever you may be
O let your wind go free
'Cos holding it caused the death of me

Obviously we should just let it **RIP**.

"Heavens, Fred, you've blown up the cow!"

Why do we fart? We look later at food and digestion and gastro-intestinal tracts, but the bottom line is: we fart because we want to. Yet this is the function of our bodies least spoken of, particularly by women. Women fart as much as men, let's face it, but do they admit it?

No, and that's a story in itself.

In 1986, the well-known American fartologist, Dr. H. K. Poltweed, carried out a survey which had some surprising results. To begin with, it showed that 97.8 per cent of men admit to farting, but only 1 per cent of women do. But 100 per cent of women, when asked if they had just farted, LIED.

Here is a table of Dr. Poltweed's findings:

	Surveyed	Say they fart	Lied..........	Actually fart	%age of total
Men	50,000	48,917	0	48,917	97.8%
Women	50,000	553	49,922	52,122	104.2%

Of course women fart, although some better than others, and many of their flatulent deeds have been recorded in the famous limericks of Olde Englande:

THE LADY FROM BUTE

~~~~~~~~

At a contest for farting in Bute
One lady's exertion was cute.
It won the diploma
For foetid aroma,
And three judges were felled by the brute.

~~~~~~~~

THE DUCHESS

~~~~~~

I sat by the Duchess at tea,
And she asked, "Do you fart when you pee?"
I said with some wit,
"Do you belch when you shit?"
And I felt it was one up to me.

~~~~~~

In the early 19th century, the *English Jest Book* recorded the following tale: A country woman who farted a great deal wants to confess this, since she enjoys it so much she feels it must be a sin. She asks the lady of the manor what is a polite word for this, and the lady, having a joke at her expense, tells her it is "committing adultery." She tells the priest she wants to confess this. "At your age?" exclaims the shocked priest. "How often do you do it?" "About thirty or forty times a day." "What does your husband say to that?" "He says: 'More power to your big, fat arse!'"

The fat lady who thought cycling might be good for her flatulence.

The venue of many a farting
joke is the gentlemen's club:

Member: "I say, old chap, do
you mind if I smoke?"
Friend: "Not at all, old boy, if
you don't mind if I fart."

Carruthers, reading the *Times* in his club, lets out a stinker. After a moment of chilling silence the chap in the next chair says: "I say, Carruthers, did you just fart?" "Of course I did," comes the scornful reply. "You don't think I smell like this all the time, do you?"

Another classic takes place at the Portsmouth sail past of the fleet, where a young lieutenant drops a doozy right in front of the brightly garlanded reviewing stand. "I say there," says the admiral, "do you know you just farted in front of my wife?" "Terribly sorry, sir," comes the unabashed reply. "I didn't realize it was her turn!"

A man complaining of persistent flatulence tells the doctor that for some strange reason his farts don't stink. "As a matter of fact," he confesses, "I've just farted twice!" The doctor gives the man some tablets, and within a few days, to the patient's surprise, his farts take on a familiar whiff. He returns to the surgery, where the doctor seems delighted. "Well, now," he says. "We've fixed your nose. Now I'll give you something for your farting."

"You're on the air in ten seconds, and remember—no 'ers' or 'ahs,' and for godsake, don't fart."

CHAPTER 2

THE SONG OF THE FART

While farting in the font one day
In the merry, merry month of May,
The vicar was repell'd
And we nearly were expell'd
For farting in the font one day.

The fart has provided endless entertainment for the composers of limericks and Rugby songs, and of course to the graffitists, and the humble authors of rhymes on dunny doors. Its range of musical tones and its concern with one of the more liberated and liberating acts of life make it a rousing and creative theme for many works of poetic art. "The Farta from Sparta" is as much a classic of the genre as "Eskimo Nell" is to another. "Port Makes Me Fart" is also flatulent doggerel of the very highest disorder.

"Harry, did you hear that?"

PORT MAKES ME FART

I'm a bit of a wine dot,
I love a good red,
And I like to drink muscat
Whilst lying in bed.
I love a fine sherry —
I'll have a good snort —
But there's one thing I do love,
A good glass of port.

CHORUS:
But FART, FART, port makes me FART.

✤

I went down to Dijon
To have a good time,
Three bottles of Champers,
And four more of wine.
I'd duck, grouse and pheasant,
Far more than I ought,
And then with me custard
Just one glass of port.

CHORUS:
But FART, FART, port makes me FART.

❖

I tried to ignore it,
To pretend it weren't there,
I tried to contain it,
And got full of air.
And then I released it
It went EVERYWHERE.

CHORUS:
But FART, FART, port makes me FART.

❧

The moral to this tale is
An ill wind blows no good.
Some get the wind from Cabernet
And some from treacle pud.
Some get the wind from radishes
Or cabbages and Kings,
But I say true flatulence
It comes from simple things.

CHORUS:
But FART, FART, port makes me FART.

The origin of the limerick is unknown, but it probably derives from the chorus of an 18th-century Irish soldiers' song, "Will you come up to Limerick?" The limerick theme was often nonsensical and frequently ribald, and farting was a popular source. The rhymingness of Sparta proved irresistible to generations of ribald limerick writers, and there are many sequels to and variations on the most famous of farting verses, "The Farta from Sparta."

THE FARTA FROM SPARTA

~~~~~~~~~~

So glib with his asshole was Carter,
No man with a mouth appeared smarter.
What issued ethereal
From that vent-hole sphinctereal,
Transcended the Farta from Sparta.

~~~~~~~~~~

THE FELLOW FROM SPARTA

~~~~~~~~~

You've heard of that fellow from Sparta
Renowned as musician and farter.
He could fart pizzicata
With flute obligata,
And the bass of Bach's B-flat toccata.

~~~~~~~~~

A YOUNG GIRL FROM LA PLATA

There was a young girl from La Plata
Who was widely renowned as a farta.
Her deafening reports
At the Argentine sports
Made her much in demand as a starta.

There were many variations on the theme, of course, and now the bibliography of farting in the limerick is practically limitless. As a living art form the limerick continues to expand the horizons of humorous and ribald writing, and the fart is carried along in the storm.

AMELIA: "I'll stop smoking if you stop farting."

A YOUNG LADY FROM BRISTOL

~~~~~~~~~

There was a young lady from Bristol
Who went to the Palace called Crystal.
She said: "It's all glass,
And as round as my arse,"
And she farted as loud as a pistol.

~~~~~~~~~

AN ECHOING FART

~~~~~~~~

It takes little strain and no art
To bang out an echoing fart.
The reaction is hearty
When you fart at a party,
But the sensitive persons depart.

~~~~~~~~

AN OLD FELLOW NAMED ART

~~~~~~~~~~

There was an old fellow named Art,
Who awoke with a terrible start,
For down by his rump
Was a terrible lump
Of what should have just been a fart.

~~~~~~~~~~

A PHILOSOPHER ONCE NAMED DESCARTES

~~~~~~~~~~

A philosopher once, named Descartes,
Was explaining himself to a tart.
"Since I think — I exist,"
He remarked as he pissed,
"But what does it mean when I fart?"

~~~~~~~~~~

AN NEFARIOUS NAZI NAMED GOEBBELS

~~~~~~~

A nefarious Nazi named Goebbels,
Once loaded his anus with poebbels.
The slightest suspicion
Or hint of sedition,
Found him farting a broadside at roebels.

~~~~~~~

HARRY: *"Did you fart, Cynthia?"*
CYNTHIA: *"Of course not. It must have been Horace."*
HORACE (Thinks): *"The sooner I get back to the front, the better."*

~~~~~~~~~

A Phony pop artist named Hart,
In a jug kept a large purple fart.
He said, "Yes, it's mine,
And I think it's divine.
Who are you to say it ain't art?"

~~~~~~~~~

AN OBSERVANT OLD CODGER NAMED BROWDER

An observant old codger named Browder
Said, "Now between bean soup and chowder,
You'll find, my good friend,
That bean soup — in the end —
Will prove to be several times louder."

A GASEOUS OLD LADDIE NAMED CARTER

Said a gaseous old laddie named Carter,
Well-known as a hell of a farter:
"It's that bad sauerkraut
That I've eaten, no doubt,
So here goes a blast for a starter."

A CRAFTY OLD BUGLER FROM RHEIMS

~~~~~~~~~

A crafty old bugler from Rheims,
Would feast upon rum chocolate creams,
Then fart a toccata
Or a Mozart sonata,
On 17th-century themes.

~~~~~~~~~

~~~~~~~~

Sir Reginald Barrington, Bart,
Went to a masked ball as a fart.
He had painted his face
Like a more private place,
And his voice made the dowagers start.

~~~~~~~~

A YOUNG FELLOW NAMED CHARTED

~~~~~~~

There was a young fellow named Charted,
Who rubbed soap on his bum when it smarted.
And to his surprise
He received a grand prize,
For the bubbles he blew when he farted.

~~~~~~~

Pickpocket to gentleman:
"Promise not to fart, sir, and I'll put it back."

CHAPTER 3

LE PETOMANE

The greatest farter the world has ever known was Joseph Pujol. He became famous as Le Petomane, the toast of Paris, a remarkable performer whose unique brand of showmanship shook and shattered the famous Moulin Rouge.

Le Petomane could fart in five keys, and although the French regarded farting as somewhat vulgar, as they do to this day, they couldn't resist the music hall act to end all music hall acts. "People were literally writhing about," wrote one theatre critic of a performance of Le Petomane early in 1890. "Women, stuffed in their corsets, were being carried out by nurses stationed in the hall, well displayed in their white uniforms. It certainly was an act."

"In the auditorium a compere playing up the incredulity would climb up on stage and announce that there was absolutely no trick, and that this outstanding artist had nothing concealed in his pants. Then the enthusiasm became delirious. It's almost impossible to imagine the noise people made who wanted to shout even louder, the apoplectic faces, the streaming tears . . . they needed a good quarter of an hour to get their breath back."

The young Pujol had a normal enough childhood, but in the summer he left school an extraordinary thing happened. He was swimming at the beach with friends when he held his breath and put his head under water. He was astonished to find that his stomach immediately filled with cold seawater through his anus. He recalled the feat several years later when he was doing his military service, and his fellow soldiers immediately wanted to know if it would happen again.

❖

On a day's leave he went down to the sea for the experiment and
to his astonishment the same phenomenon took place, and for
some time he amused his friends by ejecting all the water he had
taken in through his rectum as a waterspout. He soon found he
could take in air instead of water, and his son, Louis Pujol, wrote
later: "He would stop breathing through his nose and mouth, take
in air through his back passage and at will blow it out again with
all sorts of noise—a veritable fart fantasia—
and it was he himself who thought up the name, Le Petomane."

❖

Pujol took what he called his musical anus to Paris in 1892 and became an outrageous hit at the Moulin Rouge at a time when other stars of Parisian show-biz included Sarah Bernhardt, Rejane, Lucien Guitry and Yvette Guilbert. Le Petomane made more money for his appearances than any of them. He presented himself with an ease of good humor that worked beautifully on the public: "Ladies and gentlemen, I have the honor to present a session of Petomanie. The word *Petomanie* means someone who can break wind at will but don't let your nose worry you. My parents ruined themselves scenting my rectum!"

❖

During the initial silence he would begin a series of small farts, naming each one: "This is a little girl, this the mother-in-law, this the bride on her wedding night (very little) and the morning after (very loud), this the mason (dry—no cement), this the dressmaker tearing two yards of calico (this one lasted at least ten seconds and imitated to perfection the sound of material being torn), then a cannon (Gunners stand by your guns! Ready—fire!), the noise of thunder, etc., etc."

✤

"Then," wrote young Pujol, "my father would disappear for a moment behind the scenes to insert the end of a rubber tube, such as are used for enemas. It was about a yard long and he would take the other end in his fingers and in it place a cigarette which he lit. He would then smoke the cigarette as if it were in his mouth, the contraction of his muscles causing the cigarette to be drawn in and then the smoke blown out. Finally my father removed the cigarette and blew out the smoke he had taken in.

"He then placed a little flute with six stops in the end of the tube and played one or two little tunes such as *Le Roid Dagobett* and, of course, *Au claire de la lune*. From the beginning of the 'audition' mad laughter had come. This soon built up into general applause. The public and especially women fell about laughing. They would cry from laughing. Many fainted and fell down and had to be resuscitated."

The feats of Le Petomane triggered the imagination of generations of story-tellers and imitators. In the United States it gave rise to the legend of Gustave Andre Stool, the famous farting ventriloquist who, during the late '40s and '50s, is said to have amazed audiences around the country with his ability to throw a fart across the stage and into the audience.

The famous story, as recorded by Travis W. Pacone, recounts his final performance at the second inauguration of Richard Nixon. Standing in the audience, some 100 feet from the stand, Stool threw a fart at the president right in the middle of the swearing in. At that moment the chief justice turned to a colleague, and was heard to whisper, "An ominous air hovers over this administration."

"Maggie, where the devil are you?
Fart, and give me a clue!"

CHAPTER 4

THE FARTA FROM SPARTA

Flatulent fiends come and go, but few will forget
another Petomane-style character, a hero of
generations of English Rugby clubs.
He is known simply as "The Farta from Sparta,"
and he has been immortalized in the following
stirring verse:

There was a young fellow from Sparta,
A really magnificent farter,
On the strength of one bean
He'd fart God Save the Queen
And Beethoven's *Moonlight Sonata*.

He could vary, with proper persuasion,
His fart to suit any occasion.
He could fart like a flute,
Like a lark, like a lute
This highly fartistic Caucasian.

This sparkling young farter from Sparta
His fart for no money would barter.
He could roar from his rear
Any scene from Shakespeare,
Or Gilbert and Sullivan's *Mikader*.

He'd fart a gavotte for a starter,
And fizzle a fine serenata.
He could play on his anus
The Coriolanus
Oof, boom, er-tum, tootle, yum ta-dah.

He was great in the Christmas Cantata,
He could double-stop fart the Toccata,
He'd boom from his ass
Bach's *B-Minor Mass*
And in counterpoint, *La Traviata*.

Spurred on by a very high wager
By an envious German named Bager,
He proceeded to fart
The complete oboe part
Of a Hayden Octet in B-major.

His range went from classic to jazz
On the tonic solpha of his azz,
With a good dose of salts
He could whistle a waltz
Or swing it in razzamatazz.

His basso profundo was rare
For he had very little to spare,
But his great work of art,
His fortissimo fart,
He saved for the *March Militaire*.

One day he was dared to perform
The *William Tell Overture* storm.
But naught would dishearten
Our talented Spartan,
For his fart was in wonderful form.

It went off in capital style,
As he farted along with a smile,
Then feeling quite jolly
He tried the finale
Blowing double-stop farts all the while.

The selection was tough, I admit,
But it did not dismay him one bit.
    Then, with ass thrown aloft
    He suddenly coughed . . .
And fell in a shower of shit.

His bunghole was flown back to Sparta,
Where they buried the rest of our farter,
    With a gravestone of turds
    Inscribed with the words:
"To the Fine Art of Farting, Our Martyr."

FAIR COUSIN: "You don't mean you're going to fart,
Charles, and there are strangers in the carriage?"
CHARLES: "Well, as I don't see any gentlemen among 'em to kick
up a row, I think I might as well."

CHAPTER 5

THE PHYSIOLOGY OF FARTING

There was an old doctor called Bart
Who encouraged his patients to fart.
He said the relief
Was usually brief
But terribly good for the heart.

Farting is a subject very close to the hearts of many doctors, although some of them have trouble coming to terms with the term itself. Not so the Oriental doctor who gave a European visitor the charming, and presumably accurate, diagnosis: **"You have too much farty up, and not enough farty down."**

The terminology of flatulence was given some attention several years ago in the learned journal *Verbatim*. An editorial article stated: "Dr. R. J. L. Waugh has drawn the attention of readers to the lack of any single word in the English language other than fart for the passage of rectal flatus."

Most of the bodily functions can be described by words suited to polite society of physiological terminology, for example, eructate, masticate, sternutate, micturate, defecate, copulate. But there is no corresponding word for fart, which remains taboo with a large portion of the population.

"In my lecture to the Listerian Society in this hospital on April 30, 1974, I proposed that the act of passing rectal flatus should be termed *deflatulate* in its verbal form, when a single word was needed in circumstances unsuited to a monosyllabic alternative." There is no need to say that deflatulate would get short shrift from the limerick writers, but there are plenty clever enough to sing about farts without actually mentioning the word.

AN UNFORTUNATE GIRL NAMED LOUISE

~~~~~~~

An unfortunate girl named Louise
Lets a vast ventral blast with each sneeze.
She attracts quite a crowd
When they rip out real loud
And she blushes right down to her knees.

~~~~~~~

Gertie's blown the sides out of her nightie again.

There has been a lot of guff written about what causes farting, but an interesting fact is that a fair percentage of farts occur because we talk too much. It's wind in the system, you see, and a fair bit of it is swallowed while we are eating, and the more we talk as we eat, the more air we are likely to swallow. A fair bit of this is released by belching, but the rest usually passes on down through the small intestine into the colon. The plot thickens.

✤

Colonic gas is about 50–60 per cent nitrogen and 30–40 per cent carbon dioxide. The remaining 5–10 per cent is where the venom lies, because it is made up of hydrogen sulfide, better known as rotten egg gas, methane, the stuff that makes coal mines explode from time to time, and hydrogen, one of the most flammable of all the gases. Phew, what a mixture—and all sitting there in the bottom part of your gastro-intestinal system waiting for a chance to burst upon an unsuspecting world!

Sometimes it does so with tragic results. In 1980, in a hospital in Denmark, gastro-intestinal surgeons were operating on a male patient when things went wrong in a big way. An electrical surgical knife, much favored by modern surgeons because they cauterize small blood vessels as they go, ignited a pocket of intestinal gases. This set off an explosion which rippled its way through the poor fellow's digestive organs, and despite the best efforts of the surgeons to repair the damage, the patient died.

❖

"Colonic gas is normally expelled by the act of flatulation," the *Encyclopedia Britannica* informs us. "Movement of gas in the digestive tract produces gurgling sounds known as **borborygmus**." What they really mean is that your tummy gives a great rumble, and you fart. Simple as that. It reminds us of the young man from a particular American university:

A YOUNG MAN FROM PENN STATE

~~~~~~~~

There was a young man from Penn State
Who could fart at a terrible rate.
Rips, rattles and growls
Came forth from his bowels;
He maintained it was something he ate.

~~~~~~~~

A PECULIAR YOUNG SCOT NAMED McDOUGAL

~~~~~~~

A peculiar young Scot named McDougal
Delights to break wind in a bugle.
Otherwise he is sane,
Comes in out of the rain,
Is hardworking, kindly and frugal.

~~~~~~~

In fact all the scientific stuff about bacterial action also means that what you eat also affects the way you fart. Highly spiced and very cold foods, for instance, pass more quickly through the system, and your digestive rate can also be affected if you become emotionally upset. And although the small intestine digests and absorbs most kinds of food, beans, nuts and grains are converted by bacteria into other products, and hydrogen is given off in the process.

❖

Beans, in other words, make you fart.

HEINZ MEANS FARTZ

is a famous graffito, and the campfire scene in Hollywood's
Blazing Saddles is another brilliant testament to the flatutory power
of beans. Beer and other fizzy drinks make you fart. Whipped
desserts contain tiny air bubbles, and they also eventually emerge
as farts. You just never know, do you?

It reminds us of the best definition we have heard of Cuisine Nouvelle. Two blue-vested workers were having a quiet beer at the pub.

"Me wife's funny," said one. "It was her birthday and she said she wanted to go to one of them fancy Frog restaurants. So we dressed up and off we went."

"Yeah," said his mate. "What was it like?" "Bloody expensive, though the grub wasn't too bad. But the portions were so small if you went outside and had a good fart you were hungry again."

But it's an ill wind, as they say, that blows no one some good. How did London, for example, rid itself of the worst of its bawdy houses?

A flatulent Cockney named Billy
Could fart like a two-year-old filly.
He did it so well
That he soon blew to hell
Every brothel in old Piccadilly.

CHAPTER 6

THE A–Z OF FARTING

A detailed and intimate
examination of the art of
flatulence for those people who think
a fart is just a fart.

The Absolute Rip-Snorter

This is a man's world kind of fart, the dawn buster, the volley of cannon before the blood-surging ride into the valley of death, the rat-tat-tat of the regimental drum. There's more than a hint of devil-may-care about the rip-snorter and a whiff of gunpowder too, an up-and-at-'em lads reverberation issued by sar'nt-majors before they all go over the top. Now more usually heard over pool tables in city bars, or among victorious spectators at football matches.

THE ARTISTIC FART

Sometimes heard at the ballet, as the chap in the very tight trousers hoists the girl in the frilly skirt on to his shoulder. Was it her, or him? Was it the floorboard? More pugnacious at gallery openings, particularly after the cheap bubbly and the cold sausage rolls have started to have an effect. All art is life, and life is art, and we know what rhymes with art.

The Awkward Fart

Unplanned, exertion-based farts have embarrassed us all. Getting out of chairs, sitting down on lawns, picking up ladies' purses, squeaky trousers on leather chairs, getting an extra yard at Lord's or reaching for the smash at Wimbledon, maneuvering gingerly into the dentist's chair, hauling luggage out of overhead Jumbo jet lockers, curtsying to the Queen.

THE BATHTUB FART

This is one of the very best of all farts, except, perhaps, when saving water by bathing with a friend. It is a three-dimensional fart, which is quite rare. Not only can you hear it and, well, smell it, you can actually *see* it, which can be quite exciting. Tiny bubbles, sometimes, at others a Vesuvius-like rumble followed by a tidal wave that washes the rubber ducky right out of the bath. We now know that Archimedes was a bath farter. Remember his cry of *EUREKA!!* as he sat in his bath in Ancient

Greece one day? He had discovered the principle of flotation, of course, and it all came back to him when he shifted on to his left buttock and dropped a splendid, bubbling fart. Or so the story goes. Shower farts are not as successful as bathtub farts but occasionally you can get good resonance from a loosely fitted shower screen, and farting in spas isn't much fun because the bubbly effect is lost. But for a truly spectacular underwater eruption nothing beats a visit to the zoo after the hippopotamus has finished his lunch of cabbage stalks.

See also **Z** as in Zoo Farts.

Burning Farts

This is sometimes practiced by schoolboys in the dressing room of the cricket pavilion while waiting for the rain to stop, particularly if breakfast has been baked beans on toast. The idea is for the 12th man or someone to bend over while the skipper lights a match, and then to all take notice whether the fart burns blue or yellow. If it burns red, the whole team is in trouble, and the pavilion at serious risk of losing its roof. If you are keen on experimenting with burning farts it's a good idea to have someone standing by with a bucket of water. Safe fart burning should be practiced at all times.

THE CAR FART

These can be needlessly unpleasant, particularly if you are a passenger in the back seat on a foggy night after a supper of beer and Cornish pasties. Modern technology has come to the rescue of the back seat farter, however, in the shape of the electric window winder, which allows a much more surreptitious release of effluvium than was possible with the old mechanical ones.

One driver we know who farted a lot would say jovially:
"I think we've hit a Van Dyke!"

THE CHURCH FART

You have heard the old saying: "As popular as a fart in church." And you probably remember Confucius saying: "Man who farts in church is sitting in his own pew." Both are self-explanatory, as is the "did an angel speak fart," which seems to be associated with retired clergymen who insist on sitting in the front row although they've obviously heard it all before.

THE CURRY FART

We shouldn't have to mention how dangerous this particular effusion is, particularly in India. It takes on even more dangerous connotations if you are in India and you are not Indian. Holidaymakers partaking of curry should avoid farting at all times, because dry cleaning is expensive even when it exists, and those laundry wallahs on the banks of the Hoogli beat the hell out of white chaps' trousers.

THE DOG DID IT FART

We all know dogs fart, particularly when they're in front of the fire. It's natural enough. They're usually there after their evening meal, and the warmth of the fire gets the digestive system bubbling along. Dogs are too nice to get much pleasure out of farting in front of the fire, but they get a bit upset when they're then kicked outside into the rain and cold. Particularly when they haven't done it, particularly when it's that beer-filled lout on the couch watching television who says: "It was the dog." Real dog farts can be fairly foul, but so is the behavior of those who blame their own farting on man's best friend.

Please try to be nicer. Dogs are people, too, you know.

Dad and Dave

DAD: "Don't blame the bloody dog, Dave."
DAVE: "No, Dad."

THE DOONA LIFTER FART

~~~~~~~

In northern Europe, this is better known as the Duvet Lifter, or in China as the Quilt Lifter. Whatever the geography, cause and effect is the same. Too many Brussels sprouts with the quiche Lorraine, too much mai tai with the chicken in black bean, and at around about 3 a.m., WHOOOOMBA. Sometimes the doona/duvet/quilt lands on the floor, which is unsatisfactory, particularly in winter. On the other hand doonas/duvets/quilts have strong muffling qualities, which means that you can often get away with a good post-midnight fart with hardly any consequences at all. It is a reminder also of the old saying that the honeymoon is over when your partner farts in bed.

THE EGG SANDWICH FART

Eggs and farts have a great deal in common. When an egg goes rotten it creates hydrogen sulfide, which is known, reasonably enough, as rotten egg gas. When we digest certain food the funny things going on in our stomachs also at times produce hydrogen sulfide. The so-called egg sandwich fart is therefore one of the worst possible. In fact, they can be vile. In some women the pre-menstrual variety is more like an emission of nerve gas. But that is a sexist remark, and should be struck from the record.

The Elephant Fart

For all-round timbre, complexity and sheer exuberance—simply the best. Scientists tell us that because of their eating habits and plumbing arrangements, elephants can manufacture several thousand liters of farting gas per day. Thank god they rarely eat broccoli. And thank god they're too big to be kept indoors.

THE EXCLAMATION FART

We have mentioned that Martin Luther punctuated his sermons with ripping farts. It's certainly a good way to make a point. The good exclamation fart calls for perfect timing, however, and should not be undertaken by amateurs or without plenty of practice. Otherwise you would just be fluffing your lines. Exclamation farts can also be useful if you are in the audience and the speaker is either boring you to tears or building up to a point with which you violently disagree. A good loud fart is a good attention grabber, although of course timing is again of vital importance.

THE FAIRY FART

Said to be the softest and sweetest of farts, the faintest rustle of thistledown on a summer's day, the flutter of gossamer wings, the merest honeyed whisper. Pfffft, pssseeee. It reminds us of Cecil and Cedric watching the hefty brewery worker unloading his truck. As he dumps a great keg to the ground he lets rip with a crackling fart and Cecil says to Cedric: "Oh, Cedric, a virgin."

OLD MAN (SNIFFING): "I love her free, fine, careless rapture."

THE FIRECRACKER FART

This is quite a celebratory fart, particularly noticeable during Chinese New Year when things are exploding everywhere, presumably to keep away evil spirits. The firecracker fart is thus redolent of gunpowder, chili crabs, 1,000-year-old eggs, stir-fried broccoli and crinkly cabbage. You sometimes get the feeling we would be better off with the evil spirits.

THE FRENCH FART

~~~~~~~~~

There was an old roué of Chartres
Who had to stoop over to fartre.
He'd oft burst his britches
Which put folk in stitches,
But proved most inspiring to Sartre.

THE GERMAN FART

The growl of Panzers in the western desert, the deep throaty thrum of the beer halls, the whump of sauerkraut and pickled pork, the whine of an over-revving BMW, the scream of exploding lederhosen and the plump *Ja*! of a dairy-fed fraulein. Healthy, happy, noisy. Did you know the German word for start is fahrt?

THE GREENHOUSE EFFECT FART

Scientists say the Earth is warming up, and this could have disastrous effects because the Arctic and Antarctic ice-caps would defrost, and there would be more than water on the kitchen floor. They reckon things are heating up because cattle and sheep fart too much. Do you believe that? Imagine the Martians looking down in a few million years and saying "There goes Earth. Farted to death by those silly looking sheep." In fact, the Commonwealth Scientific and Industrial Research Organisation (CSIRO) has done a lot of work on animal farts, and reckons that methane produced by cattle and sheep provides only one-third of the 5.3 million to 12 million metric tons of gases released from Australia into the atmosphere each year. So there.

THE HABITUAL FARTER

Every office has one. Wears tweed hacking jackets to better facilitate his habit, and eats hard boiled eggs, baked beans, sauerkraut, Brussels sprouts, cauliflower, pizza with sausage, onion and anchovy, all washed down with light beer. Wants, and deserves, a room of his own.

The Hangover Fart

It is fashionable in some circles to show compassion
to those not as well-off as ourselves. Not in this case.
The hangover farter deserves all the opprobrium he gets,
particularly if he's been out all night on steak Diane and
red ned. Foul beast. To be avoided at all cost. cf. habitual
farter, and other anti-social types.

THE HORSE FART

Horses fart with a fine, fair, careless rapture that puts most humans to shame. Good show jumpers, hunters and hurdlers are particularly good farters, and that's why. This reminds us of the story of the Queen, riding in her open landau with one of the African presidents, when one of her famous grays let out an enormous fart. "Oh, I do beg your pardon," said the Queen. "That's alright, ma'am," said the president. "I thought it was one of the horses."

The Icelandic Fart

There is an old saying in Iceland: "Everyone likes the smell of his own fart." The Iceland Fart, therefore, is something of an introspective fart, usually dropped so deeply within the distant reaches of a fur coat that only the owner ever gets to appreciate it. Hence the saying. This is strictly a Northern Hemisphere fart and fairly rare at that.

THE IMMACULATE FART

This is a peculiarly Christian, or, more correctly, Catholic manifestation of the flatist's art. There has been no food, no drink, no indigestion, no discomfort of the internal drainpipe system, yet you fart. This is a truly miraculous fart, and not often encountered in these wayward times. More's the pity.

THE INCENSE FART

This used to be quite common in such places as Greenwich Village and Cedar Bay where Flower People congregated to smoke funny cigarettes. Less common these days, but still noticeable in shops selling bronze gongs and cheese cloth nighties; just a whiff of something exotic in the air that has you thinking: Sandalwood? Cardamom? Rose oil? Greenhouse tomatoes? Old socks?

The Indian Farter

The Indian farter could be compared with the Indian giver (not to be confused with farting in India, see below), somewhat two-faced, slightly dishonest, none of this look you in the eye and fart stuff, underhanded, almost gratuitous. Needs telling that a fart's a fart, for all that.

Farting in India
Not to be confused with the above.
See also C, as in Curry Fart.

THE J-CURVE FART

Rare and specialized, this somewhat histrionic fart is encountered only in the hallowed halls of the Federal Treasury, particularly during recession. Not to be confused with the G-Spot Fart, which is equally rare and crops up only in obscure sex surveys. In fact, we're not entirely convinced either of them exists. Only time will tell.

The Jubilant Fart

This is also known as the Celebratory Fart. It's the pop of a good bottle of bubbly at the moment of triumph, as the world-record pole vaulter clears the bar, the weight lifter completes the snatch and jerk, the 100-foot putt drops in the hole, the man of your dreams gets down on his knees and finally proposes. It's VE Day and the World Cup Final all wrapped up into one long, reverberating BRRRRRPPPPPP of triumph and success. A gold medal, cordon bleu, nulli secundus kind of fart that lives in the memory long after the whiff has gone.

THE JUNK FART

~~~~~~

Once known as the Fish and Chip Fart, the Pie and Pastie with Sauce Fart or the Jellied Eel Fart. It now erupts upon us in many modern guises. It's the steamed dimmie fart, the tapas bar fart, the take-away Vietnamese fart, the saveloy-in-batter-on-a-stick fart, the curry puff fart and the McDonald's fart. Highly processed and brightly packaged, it is a destroyer of heritage fart not to be taken lightly. You notice them everywhere after football games, and they could well be the contributing cause of ozone-layer depletion now being widely blamed on sheep and cow farts. Is there no justice?

THE KAMIKAZE FART

Kamikaze means divine wind, but there's nothing particularly divine about the result of a Kamikaze Fart. The farter has a crazed look in his eye and he carries on farting regardless. Also known as the Suicide Fart or Killer Fart this is a bad number, and should be immediately reported to the authorities. It is reason enough for a reinstatement of gas-mask drills. No one is safe from the kamikaze farter, not even himself.

The Kookaburra Fart

Only found in Australia, the Kookaburra Fart invariably makes people laugh. It starts out going AH AH AH then moves smoothly into OO OO OO and concludes with a wonderfully long and evocative (sometimes with a touch of echo), AH AH AH AAAAAAAH. Early settlers were somewhat confounded by the Kookaburra Fart, with its overtones of eucalyptus and dead snakes, but it is now recognized as authentically Australian, and even the National Parks and Wildlife Service is getting in on the act.

SAVE THE KOOKABURRA FART posters are now available from your local Wildlife Service headquarters, so give them a call.

THE KRAFFT-EBING FART

Not to be confused with the Kraft Cheese Fart. Prof. Krafft-Ebing was a Freudian psychiatrist who believed farting was a manifestation of mother love with lumps in it (see also L. as in The Lumpy Fart). Although often proved wrong he persisted with this preposterous view, even to the extent of wearing nappies to bed at the age of 53 (see also S. as in Silly Old Fart). Even Freud (and to a lesser extent Jung) knew that a fart is a fart is a fart.

THE RULING PASSION
Johnny (as the car bumps him): "By jove, I think she farted."

THE LACKADAISICAL FART

Fairly inexcusable, really, because a fart should denote some kind of deliberate input and output. The don't care attitude of the lackadaisical farter doesn't get anybody anywhere, and could bring the whole business into disrepute. It is a kind of lounge potato snuffle fart, all wind and no substance, rather given to airs and graces, unenthusiastic, listless and feebly sentimental. If you find that you are slipping into lackadaisical farting mode get a grip on yourself and try a little harder. Faint fart never won fair lady.

THE LICORICE FART

~~~~~~

Slightly French, particularly when detected around
boulevard bars where old men sip pastis before noon.
Redolent of aniseed and antipathy. Here, where people
chew loathsome straps of black licorice as an aperient, the
Licorice Fart is altogether more aggressive, and care should
be taken. It was Plato who commended: "A little licorice for
thou bowels' sake." And he wasn't kidding.

The Life Be In It Fart

One of the few real farts given government sponsorship. Fart good, feel good is a motto now sweeping the country. Don't be a lounge lizard; get out and participate, that's the message. Farting is a people pastime, and better enjoyed in the great outdoors. Why fart in the sitting room when you can fart in a 1,900-square-mile national park? Think big.

THE MATRONLY FART

There was an old lady from Kent
Who farted wherever she went.
She went to the fair,
And dropped a few there,
So they plugged up her arse with cement.

THE MODEST FART

~~~~~~~

Also known as the Silent Fart, the Silent Knight, the
Breezer and various other names. Usually requires some
muscular control, particularly when one is in company.
Its antithesis is the Manly Fart or the Muscular Fart,
both of them much more forthcoming.

THE MUSICAL FART

~~~~~~

By definition the Musical Fart is restricted to the upper register of the tonic solfa, and it is not as rare as you might expect. It often has to do with constriction of the buttocks, such as applied by cushions in deep leather couches, so that the passage of wind is not unlike that through the reed of a soprano saxophone. Often, of course, the effect is lost because there never seems to be a tape recorder around when you need one.

THE NAMBY-PAMBY FART

Insipidly pretty, weakly sentimental, lacking vigor. Not unlike the lackadaisical fart but even less important in the scale of things. More a fluff than a fart.

The Neanderthal Fart

This one comes practically from pre-history, and is now only heard in the dressing rooms of aging rock 'n' roll stars although Rugby League scrimmages also sometimes echo to its primitive beat. In caveman days, of course, the Neanderthal Fart was more a means of communication and identification than an expression of gaseous relief, giving rise to the old concept of a fart in the dark. Caves were very much identified by smell because there wasn't much street lighting in the catacombs, and family members had to learn to recognize their parental pong. Our word *father*, of course, comes from the Neanderthal *farter*. Not to be confused with the Neopolitan Fart, which comes from eating too much ice cream.

THE NONAGENARIAN FART

Fairly rare, because you have to be in your 90s to enjoy it. An extrapolation of the adage that life begins at 40, and essentially a celebration of the agelessness of mankind. A fart is a fart whether you are 9 or 99. At 99, however, you have probably got more time to sit around and enjoy it. It is one of the reasons why old men a. look so inscrutable, and b. tend to smoke smelly pipes.

BOY: "Oh. Mummy. Have farts got lumps in 'em?"
MUM: "No dear, of course not."

THE OSTRICH FART

What you do is bury your head in the sand, and when you are satisfied no one is looking, you fart. This has also been referred to as the Only Obeying Orders Fart, or the I Didn't Know It Was Loaded Fart. It's rather like going into space with three other astronauts without telling them you have been on a diet of chili beans for three years. It's a cowardly fart, in many ways, but we're here to talk about farting, not to be moralistic. It raises an interesting question, nevertheless: Do ostriches fart?

O

THE OUTRAGEOUS FART

~~~~~~~~

These usually come in pairs. Being caught dropping the first
fart you have blown the plot, so there's no real reason not to
drop the second. Hence it could also be called the Opera Box
Fart, the Honeymoon Fart, the First Date Fart or the Job
Interview fart. It's really a to-hell-with-the-lot-of-you fart,
and you have to put up with the consequences.

THE A–Z OF FARTING 129

THE PING-PONG FART

The Ping-Pong Fart is essentially an audio fart, coming as a progression of hollow-sounding, almost onomatopoeic pings and pongs like a ping-pong ball bouncing across a table and finally falling to the floor. It is therefore a multi- tonal fart which makes it fairly rare and sought after by specialists in the field. It is thought to have been discovered in China by President Nixon, no mean farter himself (see: The Presidential Fart).

THE PRESIDENTIAL FART

Peter the Great of all the Russians is said to have been a prodigious farter, but modern leaders of the American persuasion have also developed reputations as flatus fiends. We have just mentioned Richard Nixon and his alleged discovery of the Ping-Pong Fart. Lyndon Johnson was an enthusiastic farter although he frequently blamed eruptions of his Texas chili beans on either his horse or his dog. But Gerald Ford was perhaps the best of the lot. The Washington press gallery used to joke about the president's lack of coordination, particularly late at night, and the popular saying was that Gerald Ford couldn't whistle and chew gum at the same time. This was in fact a sanitized version. The real line was: Gerald Ford can't fart and chew gum at the same time.

THE QUACK-QUACK FART

First noted by Donald Wetzel in *The Fart Book* (Ivory Tower, 1983), the Quack-Quack Fart is a silly name for a fart. A lot of people will call it the Duck Fart. But it is important to remember that this is a double-noted fart. And while quack-quack is the sound a duck makes and the sound of the Quack-Quack Fart, there is nothing to stop a duck from going quack just once, not twice. So that is why it is called the Quack-Quack Fart. Just to be exact. Fairly rare.

THE QUADRAPHONIC FART

This is perhaps the greatest of all audio farts, and because it calls for a good deal of cooperative effort it could also be called the Team Fart or the Family Fart. It is best performed in a worn, weatherboard attic, about 10 feet by 10 feet, and after a splendid meal of curry, beans, cauliflower and ice-cold beer. Team/family members sit facing the corners of the attic and the team leader/patriarch/matriarch shouts: "All together now!" and away you go. The rumbling of the beans plus the reverberation of the weatherboards can make dogs bark clear into the next suburb.

THE QUINTESSENTIAL FART

Fart: Small explosion between the legs (School Dictionary).

Fart: An anal emission of intestinal gases, especially when audible (Webster Comprehensive Dictionary).

Fart: 1. Emit from anus; fool about or around.
2. Emission of wind from anus; contemptible person
(Oxford Concise Dictionary).

Fart: Wax, as in wax skis (Collins Pocket French-English Dictionary).

Fart: Pet. (Collins Pocket English-French Dictionary).

Fart: Doris Hart (rhyming slang).

THE RIPSNORTER

Also known as the Real Fart. No hanky-panky here, no backsliding, no blaming the dog. The ripsnorter is a look-you-in-the-eye and fart fart, crisp, melodious and, inevitably, malodorous. It bears sting but no ill will, and although in evidence at football games and the races, and sometimes on the golf course, it is essentially a good pub fart. The problem is that one ripsnorter tends to beget another ripsnorter, and if you happen to be in a big school, the chances are that you will soon have to find another bar. If the barman complains about too much ripsnorting, remind him in straightforward terms of the ancient adage:

BEER MAKES ME FART.

THE ROSICRUCIAN FART

This is not, repeat not, another name for the Excruciating Fart. The Excruciating Fart should probably have a listing all its own. The Excruciating Fart, by definition, is the first fart after an operation to fix your hemorrhoids. The Rosicrucian Fart, by contrast, is almost occult in origin, a ghostly kind of fart not unlike the Dreaming Fart, which in itself is much different from the Dreamtime Fart, although the magical connotations are not entirely dissimilar. In his *Interpretation of Dreams*, Freud referred to the Dreamtime Fart as having its origins in your mother eating too much cabbage. As far as we know he didn't say anything about the Rosicrucian Fart, which may, or may not, be significant.

THE ROYAL FART

~~~~~~~~

The story goes that Edward de Vere, 17th Earl of Oxford, knelt in front of Queen Elizabeth I and let rip with a huge fart. He was so embarrassed that he exiled himself from Court for years. When he felt brave enough to return he was spotted by the Good Queen, who said: "Come forward, Sir. We have forgiven you the fart."

THE SALMAN RUSHDIE FART

Incredibly well-crafted, literate, interesting, recognized as a work of art in some parts of the world but horribly dangerous in others. Like sport and politics, farting and religion shouldn't be allowed to mix, but living as we do in a global village, it is as well to know when you are about to drop a Salman Rushdie Fart and when you are not. Despite its obvious qualities, it is a fart not to be undertaken lightly.

Rare.

THE SILLY OLD FART

In the same family of intractable as silly old buggers, fools, bastards, twits, etc., etc. They seem to pervade the upper echelons of the church and the public service, for some reason, which may have something to do with longer lunch breaks and the availability of expense accounts. But every board and committee has one, and town councils have been known to have two or even more. The silly old fart is wayward as well as flatulent, and often becomes lost on the way home. Common, and growing ever more obvious.

THE SOMERSET FART

This is quite a pleasant fart, although not when it has pips in it. It hails from Somerset (or Zummerzet in local argot), the home of real cider, where thick-eared yokels have an old saying while on their way to inebriation from too much scrumpy:

"Oi loikes zyder
Cuz zyder lead to vartin'
An vartin' leads to Merri-ment."

AT THE SHOW.

FARMER HAYKOKK

FARMER HAYKOKK (as chauffer dives under motor):
"And yet they say the city blokes don't fart."

The Taco Fart

~~~~~~

In recent years this has joined the ranks of the fast food farts, adding color and not a little zing. In Mexico the Taco Fart is an early warning manifestation of Montezuma's Revenge, and as such is like the Curry Fart in that it is not to be taken lightly. In fact, once Montezuma's Revenge has struck it is unwise to undertake any kind of farting at all unless you have a sphincter like Captain Marvel. This is a good ethnic fart, nevertheless, and should not be confused with the Tacky Fart, which has undertones of unacceptable taste and style.

THE TASMANIAN FART

There are some of these that could come under the "Silly Old . . ."
category, but the original Tasmanian Fart is steeped in history. Abel
Tasman, for example, used to boast he could fill a topsail after eating a
keg of pickled herring, and if you search the diaries of early explorers
closely you will find several references to the peculiar farting habits of
the Tasmanian tiger and the Tasmanian devil. These days, however, the
exclusive source of the authentic Tasmanian fart is a mutton bird, a foul
creature hunted at times of the year when no other food is available
in those blighted climes and which is laughingly referred to there as a
delicacy. The mutton bird fart is laden with malice and more than a little
cholesterol, and should be avoided whenever possible.

THE FART OF THE TSARS

Ivan Vasilyevich was better known as Ivan the Terrible because when he farted all of Russia trembled, and although his descendant, Pyotr Alekseyevich, was called Peter the Great he was a terrible farter too. What made the Tsars fart? Well, they lived pretty high on the hog's back, and Peter in particular loved getting drunk and getting his guests drunk too. They were fond of vodka and beer, and when a bit tiddly were known to roar "Shchy da kasha pishcha nasha," which means roughly: "Cabbage soup and kasha (a kind of porridge) is our fare." Is it any wonder they farted?

THE UBIQUITOUS FART

Also known as the Fart that Walks. The Ubiquitous Fart is simply everywhere, particularly in airport waiting rooms, department store cafeterias and underground railway stations. It varies from summer to winter, but not much. Overwhelmingly it is a blend of onions, old socks and under-irrigated armpits, and at times is mistaken, particularly in Paris, for condition l'humanite. It is nothing of the sort. It is a stale old fart, and particularly reprehensible when blended with the dying fumes of Balkan cigars.

THE UNMENTIONABLE FART

This mean little critter is invariably dropped in polite company. No one says: "Cor, who's opened her purse?" or "Crikey, has someone just died?" No one blames the cat or dog, no one comments on the squeaky floor, and although cheeks sometimes blush red and the hostess tries surreptitiously to open a window, no one has the gumption to say: "Who farted?" The Unmentionable Fart is the bane of society, and likely to remain so until a healthier attitude is taken toward the entirely natural operation of our gastro-intestinal tracts.

THE UPWARDLY MOBILE FART

Also known as the Yuppy Fart, or the yuff, for short. Increasingly encountered among the tracksuit and BMW brigade, and sometimes around backgammon tables, the yuff is usually a low-calorie kind of fart, low in cholesterol and soluble fats, and is known in other parts of the world as the Health-Food or even the Pritikin Fart. It's fairly nondescript, but a fart, nevertheless, and deserves a place in any modern compendium.

The Vaginal Fart

Not much spoken about even in liberated circles, but again a worthwhile addition to any serious compendium of this kind. Produced during sexual intercourse, usually of a passionate nature, which includes the absorption and consequent release of wind in one form or another. Known in Ancient Egypt as the Gully Breeze and elsewhere in North Africa the Khamsah, the Vaginal Fart can cause a great deal of laughter when circumstances are right. Best enjoyed by small audiences, however.

THE VALUE-ADDED FART

Not dissimilar to the J-Curve Fart, the Value-Added Fart is also encountered in the quieter reaches of the Treasury, in the board rooms of some of our larger mining companies, and even among the gurus of the Australian Wool Board. It's not so much making something out of nothing—such as reversing the social order by claiming that you and not the dog had farted—but of seeing the possibilities of a quite ordinary fart and then processing it into something that could even be sold overseas. The possibilities are endless, and should be given very great thought at the highest possible levels. Who knows? The recession could even have a fart-led recovery.

THE VOLKSWAGEN FART

Farting in cars is bad news at the best of times, but farting in a Volkswagen is unsociable in the extreme. The Volkswagen Fart is therefore one of the worst of the genre, and is to be discouraged. We have been preaching the simple right of all, which is to fart when and where you feel like it, but farting in the back seat of a Veedub simply isn't fair.

The Whale Fart

A great deal of research had to be undertaken in some pretty unpleasant places to find out whether whales really farted or not, and the jury is still out on one or two particular species. The consensus, however, is that blue whales fart and sperm whales fart, and although no one got close enough to establish the fact beyond reasonable doubt, it is probable that killer whales fart too. During their research, however, our intrepid investigative divers noticed bubbles coming from the rear of a Russian nuclear submarine, so in later volumes of this work we may be able to expand on the Nuclear Submarine Fart.

THE WHISPER FART

~~~~~~

This is one of the genre of undercover farts, requiring good muscular control and more than a little spite. You can whisper fart your way through all kinds of situations, but eventually you'll be caught. It's more devious than the Silent Knight Fart, which often as not is an unconscious act, and it could even signal a serious personality disorder. The dedicated whisper farter should really have it seen to, but probably won't.

THE WINERY FART

See Chapter 2, "Port makes me fart." Otherwise: the know-it-all visitor to the cellar door who insists on the winemaker opening his best cabernet sauvignon, then leaving with not so much as a bottle of blackberry nip. He is second only to the hydrogen sulfide fart, which is banned these days in all but the most primitive wineries.

The Xanthic Fart

Rare, but perhaps the worst fart of all. Xanthic acid is yellowish and deeply evil, and its effects on metals such as sodium are revolting. The Xanthic Fart makes the Rotten Egg Fart smell like Chanel No. 5. One whiff of this little mover can leave you doubled over the kitchen sink for hours. It is probably an ingredient of nerve gas, which means the Xanthic Farter could well be banned by the Geneva Convention. And rightfully so. Anyone detecting a Xanthic Fart should immediately contact the Environmental Protection Agency in your nearest city. If you are well enough, that is.

THE XMAS FART

Any fart dropped at Christmas. It's a pretty productive time of year for farting, what with one thing and another, and some good variations on the theme lace scholarly works on this happiest of Christian festivals. "Fart, the herald angels sing," is an historic carol, and one presumably based on the flatulent ferocity of good King Wenceslas every time he mixed Christmas pudding and port. And how do you think fat old Father Christmas gets back up all those chimneys so quickly?

THE X-RATED FART

Certainly not for general exhibition, the X-Rated Fart invariably emerges from within the folds of dirty raincoats and is usually encountered at dirty picture shows and dirty bookstalls. In itself it is not a particularly unusual fart, but its ambience tells the story.

SMITH'S WEEKLY, 1929
Tragedy of the Flapper and the Backfire

THE YACHTSMAN'S FART

Not dissimilar to the Ripsnorter, the Yachtsman's Fart is crisp and decisive, like someone ripping a sheet of two-pound canvas. It is the result, usually, of too much beer and red beans (prairie strawberries the American cowboys used to call them), or in the old days, salt cabbage and rum, and correspondingly pungent. Keep upwind.

The Yoga Fart

The generally unpublicized cause of spontaneous levitation. The yogi feasts for many days on lentils, and forswears any relief until the mystical, magical moment when flatulence takes over and he, cross-legged and concentrating like crazy, rises into the air like a Harrier jump-jet. Action and reaction, as Newton observed, are equal and opposite, and here we have the bum acting as a launching pad. Most people believe demonstrations of levitation are faked, but they probably don't appreciate the inner power that the simple lentil can generate.

THE ZOO FART

All zoos are really a collective fart, and is it any wonder? Imagine it: elephants, hippopotamuses, rhinoceroses, buffaloes, lions, tigers, three-toed sloths, bandicoots, crocodiles and red-bummed monkeys all locked in together, eating and farting to their hearts' content. Cognoscenti take blindfolded tours these days to guess which particular cage they are standing in front of. Like wine judges they sniff and pout, then deliver their judgment. Debate still rages on whether or not birds fart.